PROSPECTING
The Key to Sales Success

Virden J. Thornton

A FIFTY-MINUTE™ SERIES BOOK

CRISP PUBLICATIONS, INC.
Menlo Park, California

PROSPECTING
The Key to Sales Success

Virden J. Thornton

CREDITS
Editor: **Robert Racine**
Managing Editor: **Kathleen Barcos**
Typesetting: **ExecuStaff**
Cover Design: **Carol Harris**
Artwork: **Ralph Mapson**

Copyright 1994 by Crisp Publications, Inc.

Printed in the United States of America

English language Crisp books are distributed worldwide. Our major international distributors include:

CANADA: Reid Publishing Ltd., Box 69559-109 Thomas St., Oakville, Ontario, Canada L6J 7R4. TEL: (905) 842-4428, FAX: (905) 842-9327

Raincoast Books Distribution Ltd., 112 East 3rd Avenue, Vancouver, British Columbia, Canada V5T 1C8. TEL: (604) 873-6581, FAX: (604) 874-2711.

AUSTRALIA: Career Builders, P. O. Box 1051, Springwood, Brisbane, Queensland, Australia, 4127. TEL: 841-1061, FAX: 841-1580

NEW ZEALAND: Career Builders, P. O. Box 571, Manurewa, Auckland, New Zealand. TEL: 266-5276, FAX: 266-4152

JAPAN: Phoenix Associates Co., Mizuho Bldg. 2-12-2, Kami Osaki, Shinagawa-Ku, Tokyo 141, Japan. TEL: 3-443-7231, FAX: 3-443-7640

Selected Crisp titles are also available in other languages. Contact International Rights Manager Suzanne Kelly at (415) 323-6100 for more information.

Library of Congress Catalog Card Number 93-73211
Thornton, Virden J.
Prospecting: The Key to Sales Success
ISBN 1-56052-271-2

This book is printed on recyclable paper with soy ink.

ABOUT THIS BOOK

Prospecting: The Key to Sales Success is not like most books. It stands out in an important way. It is not a book to read—it is a book to *use*. The "self-paced" format and many worksheets encourage readers to get involved and try new ideas immediately.

We hope that this book on prospecting will be a helpful and practical tool for you as you pursue excellence in sales. But perhaps even more important, we hope it is a book to which you can refer again and again. It is not a book to be read and put aside, but one which continues to refresh you and promote even greater productivity.

Prospecting: The Key to Sales Success can be used effectively in a number of ways. Here are some possibilities:

► **Individual Study.** Because the book is self-instructional, all that is needed is a quiet place, committed time and a pencil. By completing the activities and exercises, you receive both valuable feedback and action steps for improving the effectiveness of your sales strategy.

► **Workshops and Seminars.** This book was developed from hundreds of interactive seminars and contains many exercises that work well with group participation. The book is also a refresher for future reference by workshop attendees.

► **Remote Location Training.** This book is an excellent self-study resource for managers, supervisors and managerial candidates not able to attend "home office" training sessions.

Even after this book has been used for training and applied in real situations, it will remain a valuable source of ideas for reflection.

iii

ABOUT THE AUTHOR

As founder, president and a senior advisor at The $elling Edge®, a training and development firm in Cleveland, Ohio, Virden Thornton has assisted thousands of sales and service professionals in generating more business for their organizations. His clients include Eastman Kodak, P & C Bank, National Associates, Inc., Dean Whitter, IBM, Bolanis Financial Planning Group, Inc., and New York Life. Virden is the author of an acclaimed self-directed learning series of sales, telemarketing and motivational guides. He is a dynamic national speaker and regularly conducts workshops on sales, customer service and motivational topics.

PREFACE

Several years ago, *Sales and Marketing Management* Magazine published a list of ten books on selling that were considered by its readers (sales managers) to be the best. At the time, I owned four of the books listed. I then purchased and read the other six books and several additional selections. When I was asked by Michael Crisp to write a book on prospecting, I naturally went to these sources to see what the masters had to say. I was surprised at how little had been written about the subject. Some authors didn't even address this vital element in the sales process. Those who did excluded or only touched lightly on the most important techniques that make the difference between success and failure in selling.

When I started this project, I was concerned that it would just be a rehash of what had gone before. I asked myself, what could I possibly write in this Fifty-Minute Series that would not be found in a dozen other books on selling? I realize now that it is one of the few sources available that attempts to cover the topic in some detail.

As a sales manager, consultant and trainer, I have found that the lack of consistent prospecting is the root cause of many business and professional failures. The ideas presented here, if followed on a regular basis, can prevent this failure and set the stage for a successful professional or selling career.

Virden Thornton

DEDICATION—

This book is dedicated to David Devos, my first, and by far my best, sales manager. His focus on instilling solid prospecting skills in his staff gave me a foundation on which to build a successful career in sales. It is also dedicated to my wife, Barbara, for over thirty years of loving support.

CONTENTS

INTRODUCTION

A few years ago, a National Ad Council commercial displayed a new mouse trap. After exhibiting the trap's superior features, the ad declared, "Nothing happens until somebody sells something!" This TV spot clearly illustrated that selling is vital to the success of even an exceptional product or service. However, even selling requires a preceding step: *Nothing happens until someone does some prospecting.*

Prospecting is vital to sales success. Without a systematic method of finding customers, a company will rarely produce a steady stream of sales. Service firms (attorneys, financial planners, accountants, engineers, etc.), must also prospect regularly to attract new clients.

25 = 5 = 1

On average, you must talk to 25 suspects, *people you have never talked to before,* to locate five prospects—suspects you have screened—to make one sale. To most professionals, anyone could be a suspect. However, it is much better to target likely or potential suspects than to use a "shotgun," or scattered, approach, such as written advertising or "cold-calling."

A prospect needs your product (service), is willing to take time to learn more about your offer, or did not tell you "No." Once you have spoken with a prospect, you can then rate how likely it is that he or she will become a customer (client):

PROSPECT-RATING SCALE

A = High Potential
B = Moderate Potential
C = Minimum Potential

Use the scale to classify your existing customers (clients) as well. Using this scale, strive to meet the following goals:

GOAL #1: Maximize your contact time with your A prospects and customers.

GOAL #2: Work to convert your B prospects and customers to A's.

Obviously your C's should not take much of your valuable selling time. That does not mean you forget your "C"s. Instead, invest no more time and effort in these contacts than will produce positive results.

GOAL #3: Strive for above average results in all your prospecting activities.

Identifying Qualified Prospects

The following checklist will help you identify the difference between suspects and qualified prospects (decision makers).

Characteristics of a Qualified Prospect

1. *Has a need or a problem* that can be met or resolved by purchasing your products (services).

2. *Sees the need or problem and is willing to take action.*

3. *Is willing to consider* your products (services) as a solution to his or her problems or needs.

4. *Can afford to purchase* your products (services).

5. *Has the authority to spend money* to purchase your products (services).

Many nonproductive salespeople and service professionals fail to understand the difference between a suspect and a *qualified prospect* or decision maker. Often, the prospects they continue to pursue have one or more of the elements in the checklist missing or do not even have authority to spend money for the products or services being promoted.

Now, take a few minutes to assess your own prospecting skills.

Personal Assessment

1. I have a set schedule for prospecting on a daily and weekly basis, and I adhere to this schedule. Rank yourself on a scale of zero (never) to ten (always).

   _____

2. I use a card file, day planner or computer tracking software to effectively track and follow through on leads. (Nothing = 0; scraps of paper = 3; card file = 5; day planner = 7; and computer = 10)

   _____

3. I regularly plan my sales calls using maps to eliminate unnecessary travel time. Rank yourself on a scale from zero (never) to ten (always).

   _____

4. I use a series of softening mailers to make each appointment call as effective as possible. Rank yourself on a scale of zero (never) to ten (often).

   _____

5. I regularly ask for referrals from (list the number of sources circled). Give yourself 1 point for each item circled.

   a. Seasoned customers (clients)
   b. Prospects who say no
   c. New customers or clients who say yes
   d. Other noncompeting sales representatives
   e. Family, friends and acquaintances
   f. Vendors, accountants, attorneys and consultants
   g. Competitors
   h. Past customers
   i. Other employees and staff members
   j. Other _____

   _____

6. A good percentage of my business contacts comes from referrals. (0% = 0; 1–5% = 3; 6–10% = 5; 11–15% = 7; and 16–100% = 10)

   _____

7. Rate your call reluctance level on a scale of zero (high) to ten (none).

   _____

xi

8. I always sell an appointment, *not* my products (services), when I make appointment calls. Rank yourself on a scale of zero (never) to ten (always).

   _____

9. I give people permission to say no, and I always screen my leads to make certain I am working with someone who can make a buying decision. Rank yourself on a scale of zero (never) to ten (always).

   _____

10. I am active in my customers' (clients') trade associations as a member or associate member. Rank your activity on a scale from zero (none) to ten (high).

    _____

    _____ **Total**

There are many elements in prospecting that could make the difference in your success or failure as a sales or service professional. The ten activities just measured are a small sampling of some of these key elements.

SCORE	
91–100	You should have written this book and don't need to read further (you might get bored).
81–90	You have a good grasp of the rules and are playing the game to your advantage, but one can always use a few more ideas to improve the score.
71–80	You are using some of the tools that could make you a success, but you need to apply more of them to become a top sales producer.
51–70	You are new to the game or never really understood the rules. You need to practice the concepts outlined here.
50 or below	This book will help you get in the game and stay in until you become one of the top professionals who consistently produce high profit margins for your organization.

PART

1

Find Prospects in Published Materials

PREVIEW CHECKLIST

Read each question and check the appropriate box.

	Yes	No
1. I can list at least five sources of prospects available in published materials.	☐	☐
2. I always use at least three of those sources.	☐	☐
3. I know who to contact when need I special reference material.	☐	☐
4. I make use of the resources at my local library.	☐	☐
5. I have used the reverse phone directory to locate a decision maker.	☐	☐
6. I use the *Yellow Pages* constantly as a prospecting resource.	☐	☐
7. I have ready access to trade publications and use them.	☐	☐
8. I have tried prospecting using mailing lists in the past 60 days.	☐	☐
9. I know what SDRS stands for, and I have used the service.	☐	☐
10. I know the four important criteria to look for when selecting a list broker.	☐	☐

If you checked even one "no" box, then you are not as familiar with published prospecting resources as you could be.

CULTIVATE REFERENCE SPECIALISTS

One of the most important appointments you can make is with the reference specialist at your local library. Hard work alone will not produce positive sales results. *Learn to work smart.* Working smart means cultivating relationships with reference librarians who can help you research the market you serve to pinpoint prospective customers or clients. Learn how much they can help you under their job description and how much time they will spend on a given assignment. These relationships could prove invaluable in locating decision makers who can assist you in making your business development goals.

If you live in a location where you have access to more than one public library, cultivate relationships with a research librarian at each library. This will help you avoid overloading one librarian with your research requests.

By making friends with and getting to know individual librarians, over the long term, you will be able to rely on them to help with all your research projects. Often these professionals will go far beyond the parameters of their job once they view you as their friend.

Like most public employees, rarely do librarians receive recognition or appreciation for their effort. Remember that a *hand-written note of thanks* can go a long way toward producing more concise and extensive research reports. A recognition letter to the reference librarian's supervisor (praising a job well done) can also reinforce and enhance your working relationship. Often these small acts will produce a research assistant—one that most major corporate executives would envy—dedicated to helping you meet your goals.

By enlisting the help of others, you can more readily focus on prospecting and sales activities. Making appointments to meet reference specialists is an example of how you can cultivate a relationship that will improve your prospecting activities.

THERE IS A DIRECTORY FOR ALMOST EVERY PROSPECTING NEED

DIRECTORIES AS SOURCES FOR LEADS

Virtually hundreds of directories published in the United States contain information about the people and locations necessary for successful prospecting. Locate a public library with an extensive business section (usually in the more affluent communities) and you are well on your way to finding the information you need. You can cross-reference your findings from one source with another directory to fine-tune your research and locate just the right person or business. Most directories publish annual editions, so you can always work with the latest information. There is also a directory of directories available to locate just the right source of information. (See the Appendix for a list of the directories.)

Use the *Yellow Pages*®

For business-to-business prospecting, the single best source for finding the most successful or largest businesses in dozens of different industries is the Yellow Pages. It lists every small- to medium-sized business. You can find the yellow pages of most major cities in your state and throughout the United States stored on microfiche at your local library. If you want to own a copy, you can call your local telephone company and they will provide you with directories from your area or the telephone numbers for obtaining books from cities outside your immediate calling area or state.

Since it costs money to place an ad in the book, generally only those businesses that find yellow page advertising to be profitable continue to place ads. Also, those businesses that are new and growing, or are large enough to handle additional business, will purchase the larger ads. It is not always true that the firms listed are the most successful. However, working with those businesses that purchase larger ads is one way to find prospects that need and will buy your products (services). By comparing new and previous editions, you can also find businesses that are running ads for the first time or larger ads this time around, which may indicate successful businesses with a greater need for the products (services) of outside vendors.

DIRECTORIES AS SOURCES FOR LEADS (continued)

Trade Publications Produce Leads

Almost every industry produces a newsletter or publication for those working in a given field. Trade publications often list members or contain articles by them that can give you insight into a specific industry. Trade associations also publish membership directories. For example, the insurance claims profession directory lists:

- Insurance defense attorneys
- Hospitals
- Independent adjusters
- Appraisers
- Adjuster's company rosters
- Accounting
- Banking
- Insurance
- Legal professions

Once you determine who might want to buy your products or services, chances are there is a trade publication about, or a listing of, the people you would like to reach.

If you can not locate the material in the reference or business section of your local public library, call the industry association for more information. Sometimes there is a small charge for the guides or publications, but the cost is nominal when compared with their value in helping you achieve your promotional goals.

Exercise: Identify Trade Publications

What trade publications do you now know that serve your market?

_____

_____

_____

Government Information Services

All local, state and federal government agencies keep records on businesses and individuals under their jurisdiction. For example, city government keeps a number of useful records in the county clerk's office, including:

- construction permits
- birth records
- deeds
- marriage records
- new businesses
- leases

Most states publish numerous directories that are available at no cost. Among the most helpful are state offices regulating:

- banking
- commerce
- franchises
- insurance
- motor vehicles

The federal government has many sources of information for those professionals willing to take the time to learn about what is obtainable. Most of these sources are available through the U.S. Government Printing Office (see the Appendix for contact information). You can also find many of these sources in the reference section of your local public library.

DIRECTORIES AS SOURCES FOR LEADS (continued)

On-line Databases

If you own or have access to a computer with a modem, another great source of information is an on-line database. Standard & Poor's ratings of businesses are available on-line as well as information on Dun & Bradstreet. Most of these databases can be tapped through CompuServe and Prodigy. These services contain many useful information sources, such as Dow Jones, Mead Data Central and Lexis, which is useful if you are in the legal profession. One successful professional organization subscribes to CompuServe and every day checks the executive newswire service for stories about layoffs in major industries. This financial planning firm realizes that it is difficult to buy a mailing list of people who are contemplating early retirement. By checking which companies are downsizing, they can then obtain a list of a firm's corporate executives and target those people who may have a need for their retirement services.

Exercise: Locate Prospects

Place a check next to each source you are currently using to locate prospects.

- ☐ Reference Specialists
- ☐ Directories
- ☐ Yellow Pages
- ☐ Trade Publications
- ☐ Government Information Services
- ☐ On-line Databases

If you checked only one or two sources, you may need to expand your resources.

FIND PROSPECTS THROUGH MAILING LISTS

The main reason for buying a mailing list is to save time in trying to reach just the right group of people. In the prospecting numbers game, time is money. The more time you spend screening suspects, the less time you have for the vital business of selling and closing sales. When you value your time, using a mailing list is an economical source of names. Choosing the right list can be a critical factor in your success, but for most people it is a frightening task. *Not all mailing lists are created equal.* Be sure to check these important elements in choosing an effective list:

- List source

- Frequency of updates

- Track record

One way to overcome this problem is to locate a good list broker.

A list broker can discriminate between a list's strengths and weaknesses. A good broker can tell you:

✓ If the owner of the list has changed his or her list source

✓ If the bulk of the names on the list are new

✓ If the list contains real clients or just prospects

How do you find just the right mailing list? Or where do you locate a good list broker? These questions are what this section of the book is all about.

Start with the Standard Rate and Data Service

The *Standard Rate and Data Service* (SRDS) lists over 180 mailing list management firms. It includes close to twelve hundred lists in its extensive directory. Arranged by type of contact, it can be your starting point to locate just the right group of decision makers or companies for your products or services. Each list manager represented in the SRDS has its own strengths and weaknesses, but with a little experimentation you can find a broker who will provide you with the right target group. Most large public libraries will have the SRDS in their reference section.

FIND PROSPECTS THROUGH MAILING LISTS (continued)

Selecting a Good List Broker

What should you look for specifically when selecting a list broker?

► Personal integrity

► Honesty

► Intelligence

► Experience in your specific field

If you sell on a business-to-business basis, find a broker who has lists that can produce business contacts. If you sell to consumers, find a firm that specializes in this type of list. The broker you choose should:

1. Be able to quickly explain your list options and the historical data used to make the proposals.

2. Be prepared to negotiate the best possible rates for your situation.

3. Help with response analysis and the merging and purging of the lists you choose.

4. Become a valued advisor in the same way that you use a good attorney, accountant or stockbroker.

5. Provide the names of satisfied customers as a reference source.

You can find a broker by looking under Mailing Lists in the Business-to-Business Yellow Pages or by calling your local direct marketing club or the Direct Marketing Association in New York. See the Appendix for a list of brokers who have a good reputation.

Buying the Right Lists

Before you buy a list, you must first know your market. If you sell to consumers, you need to profile your customer (create a description such as sex, age, education, income and lifestyle). Once you have the description in mind, look for sources of lists made up of individuals with the same characteristics. After finding the source, consider testing the list by buying a small quantity first, then purchase the rest when you know it will work for you.

Business lists differ from consumer lists since you must first locate the company name and address, and then the name and title of the decision maker you wish to contact. It is easy to find lists of the businesses you wish to reach. However, changes occur so often in business today that it is difficult to get accurate lists of individual names. With business lists, you have the choice of buying a compiled list or a response list.

 ▶ **Compiled lists** usually are the least expensive. Characterized by having good coverage of a market, these directories do not usually include individual names.

 ▶ **Response lists** are those made up of individuals who have responded to a variety of direct offers. While usually composed of high-quality names, these lists don't cover the market as well as a compiled list does.

Be sure to ascertain if you are actually "buying" the list or just renting it. Most firms offer a list on a rental basis. If you want a mailing list for multiple uses, discuss what options you have with your broker. Remember, it is unlawful to copy or use a rented list beyond your original agreement without consent from the broker or owner.

Exercise: List Brokers

True   **False**

☐   ☐   1. The first place to look for a broker is the SRDS.

☐   ☐   2. A broker should have personal integrity, honesty and intelligence.

☐   ☐   3. A good broker is not expected to negotiate possible rates.

☐   ☐   4. A broker should be a trusted advisor.

☐   ☐   5. A broker should not be expected to provide the name of other customers as references.

PART

2

Person-to-Person
Prospecting

PREVIEW CHECKLIST

Check your knowledge of prospecting.

	True	False
1. In joining a trade group or association, you should stay in the background so you don't offend the membership in any way.	☐	☐
2. To make yourself known at trade shows, you should remember to bring a good supply of handout material.	☐	☐
3. The primary reason to attend a trade show is to keep up with the competition.	☐	☐
4. At a trade show, you should place the literature at the back of the booth.	☐	☐
5. You should give referrals to get referrals.	☐	☐
6. You should avoid political activity when actively prospecting.	☐	☐
7. A small, formal network works best for producing high-quality leads.	☐	☐
8. Asking for referrals is difficult for many sales representatives or service professionals.	☐	☐
9. It is risky to seek out dissatisfied clients who have quit doing business with your organization.	☐	☐
10. Competitive organizations can be a good source of leads.	☐	☐

Answers: 1. F 2. F 3. F 4. T 5. T 6. F 7. F 8. T 9. F 10. T

SEARCH OUT YOUR CENTERS OF INFLUENCE

In each community there are people who can lead you directly to prospects and sales. We sometimes call these people centers of influence (COIs). A COI could be your local banker. Bankers know a lot of people. They associate with retailers, other financial professionals, wholesalers, contractors, car dealers, distributors and a host of other business executives. They know who is going out of business and closing their doors as well as the most stable and successful business people in town.

By developing an association with a banker, attorney, accountant, financial planner or government official, you can produce a number of prospects and sales that would take years of cold canvassing to generate. A COI will vary according to the products or service that you offer. Take time to think about the people most likely to be COIs in your field; then cultivate them as members of your network to produce introductions and referrals to their base of contacts.

Exercise: Find Your COIs

List five possible COIs in your community. Place a check next to those you have as part of your network.

☐ _____

☐ _____

☐ _____

☐ _____

☐ _____

Consider contacting those whom you did not check.

NETWORK TO GET REFERRALS

Through networking contacts, you can produce a steady flow of qualified prospects. Generally qualified prospects will come from networking more than from other sources. Since both parties want to generate long-term relationshps from the leads exchanged, they usually qualify their referrals before passing them along. They know that giving out unqualified leads can lead to receiving poor-quality referrals in return, or worse, being cut off from an important lead source altogether.

CASE STUDY: GIVE AND GET

In a recent consultation, a radical strategy was proposed to help a regional financial planning firm produce more business. The company was told to put its professional service vendors on notice: Attorneys and accountants working for the firm would no longer receive leads from the firm until they began giving referrals in return. Some senior executives felt that the competence of a lawyer or accountant should be the only factor in selecting professionals to service the firm's planning clients with estate or tax problems. When these executives were asked if there were no competent professionals in the large cities that the firm served who could also provide referrals, the executive committee reconsidered their position.

They established a new policy for selecting and maintaining a list of professional vendors. A vendor must regularly give referrals to the firm to receive business in return.

Use Formal and Informal Networks

The suggestion to the executive committee is an example of a formal networking arrangement, since both the planning firm and its vendors generate business from their "formal" association. Some forms of networking are not this formal. The prior arrangement the attorneys and accountants had with the firm before the suggested change was an informal approach (even though it was one-sided favoring the vendors).

NETWORK TO GET REFERRALS (continued)

Ideas for Maintaining Solid Network Connections

▶ Give referrals to regularly receive referrals.

▶ Qualify the leads you give out and maintain a high level of quality in all your leads.

▶ Associate with as many people as you can, on both a formal and an informal basis, who can generate leads in return for your referrals.

▶ Send a hand-written note of thanks, whether you make a sale or not, when you receive a referral from an associate in your network.

▶ Keep track of casual contacts and members of your network who regularly give you leads. Cultivate these relationships even further through a scheduled contact plan, written notes, and information.

▶ Take a potential network member to lunch periodically.

▶ Treat contacts who provide you with leads like your best customers or clients. Send them birthday and anniversary cards, notes and news articles to keep your association alive and active.

▶ Maintain a large network of formal and informal referral sources so you don't have to apply pressure to a small group of people for leads.

GETTING REFERRALS: JUST ASK

Asking for referrals seems to be extremely difficult for many sales representatives and most service professionals. However, successful professionals have learned that asking for referrals is a quick and easy way to generate qualified prospects and establish a network of COIs.

Locate Additional Sales Leads Just by Asking

1. Ask Your Present Customers (Clients) for Referrals

To set the stage for obtaining referrals from customers (clients), you first need to make a "user call"—a meeting to see how they feel about the products (services) received from your organization. Never try to sell anything in a user call; just sincerely ask how your contacts feel about you.

For customers that are enthusiastic about your association, ask them to give you a letter on their stationery that will tell other people about their good feelings. Asking for an endorsement letter from customers (clients) is a good way to get them to focus on their positive relationship with you and your organization. The easiest way to obtain endorsement letters is to:

- Write them for your customers (clients), based on the discussion in your user calls.

- Once you have been given permission, you should produce letters that they can transcribe on their own stationery to save them time.

- In a cover note, let them know they can modify your draft in any way.

After receiving endorsement letters from your customers (clients), call back to see if they know someone who would benefit from learning more about your products (services), someone you could send their letter to. Customers (clients) rarely will take the time to think about your company or firm. They might even take you for granted unless you occasionally remind them of how you benefit them. For most customers (clients), asking for endorsement letters and referrals is a positive experience that will strengthen your relationship.

GETTING REFERRALS (continued)

2. Ask Disgruntled or Dissatisfied Customers (Clients) for Referrals

Develop a list of customers who no longer buy your products (services), as well as those who seem less than excited about your organization. *A successful sales professional is the one who is willing to do what the unsuccessful sales person is not willing to do.* Top sales producers know there is a good chance that, if asked, some of those disgruntled customers would come back. Successful professionals ask! The unsuccessful person assumes there is nothing to be done about past problems, so why ask?

Often, dissatisfied people feel slighted in some way or think they can get better prices elsewhere only to learn that your products (services) were far superior to those they now use, and less expensive in the long run. Still, pride can keep customers (clients) from calling you for an order or more service. By telling your contacts that you miss working with them and would like to do business again, there is a good chance they will reconsider an earlier decision. Since *returning* customers (clients) know for certain your products and services are superior, they also make good referral sources. Don't forget to ask for leads.

A smart and successful sales professional knows that dissatisfied clients should be encouraged to verbally express themselves. They want to be listened to and have their complaints taken seriously. When you respond politely and professionally to their concern, you gain their confidence and give them a reason to do business with you or your organization again.

3. Ask New Customers for Referrals

New customers (clients) are always a good source of referrals. Once they have made the decision to purchase your products (services) like religious converts, they often want to reinforce their decision by telling others about you.

One of the best ways to obtain referrals from new customers is to set the stage as you close the sale. When you discuss how much your products or services cost, merely tell your prospects that you get paid in two ways.

- First, outline the costs of your products or services and the terms for payment.

- Next, tell them that, after several months, their level of satisfaction with your products (services) will be so high that they will want to give you the names of a few people who would appreciate receiving the same benefits they have found.

4. Ask Suspects and Prospects Who Say No for Referrals

Many of the suspects and prospects who tell you no feel guilty about not being able to work with you. To help them ease their consciences, ask each of them to give you the names of people who might have a need for your products (services). Even if contacts can't or won't work with you, they may know of others who do have a need for what you sell.

5. Ask Your Competitors

Look for ways to get business from the overflow work of the large competitive firms in neighboring areas. Competitive firms can be a great source of business. Take on engagements for large competitors who don't have your specific expertise or the time to devote to a given project.

6. Ask Family, Friends and Acquaintances

Remember, *you don't know who people know*. You also may not know about a person's family relationships. People have affiliations with others through family and friends that could be of benefit to you as you prospect.

7. Ask Staff Members

Don't overlook the people with whom you work to provide you with leads.

8. Ask Your Vendors, Suppliers and Professional Consultants

The people who service your organization may have relationships with decision makers in the firms or companies to which you are trying to sell. Ask your accountant, attorney, interconnect company representative—even your photocopy machine sales representative—for referrals.

GETTING REFERRALS (continued)

9. Ask Other Sales Representatives

Noncompetitive sales professionals are an excellent source of referrals. Ask them for information about the type of person or company you are seeking and learn the type of customer they are looking for. By consistently giving them referrals, you create a need within for them to reciprocate. Over time you will develop a large network relationship that can produce a steady flow of business from other sales or service professionals.

10. Ask Total Strangers

Often you will meet someone for the first time at a cocktail party, business meeting or social gathering. Invariably the conversation turns to what you both do for a living. Such strangers may have a need for your products (services) or will know someone who does. Don't hesitate to ask:

- A stranger on an airplane

- New members of your congregation, temple or parish for the name of someone you might introduce to your products or services.

All people can do is tell you no or that they cannot think of anyone right then. But who knows, they might just give you the biggest lead of your career.

11. Ask People Who Are Referred for Referrals

Each person referred to you can also be a source for additional contacts, whether or not the referred party becomes one of your customers (clients).

Out of the eleven possible referral sources, list those that you have yet to contact. Begin cultivating them into your network as soon as possible.

_____

_____

_____

_____

_____

Ask Specifically

To avoid hearing "I can't think of anyone right now" when you ask for a referral, help your contacts identify specific individuals by describing exactly the type of person you are looking for. When you ask specifically for a firm with ten to thirty employees and over $1 million in sales that could use a specific product or service, it helps your contacts to locate that type of person, business or situation in their subconscious mind. Always ask for referrals, and always ask specifically for what it is you want.

Ask Often

Once people have given you referrals, ask them for additional contacts. *One of the biggest problems a sales professional must overcome is forgetting to ask for referrals.* By establishing a referral action plan and regularly requesting referrals from your network, you should begin to develop a steady flow of qualified prospects.

Although not all industries or products lend themselves well to offering finder's fees or commissions, in the right industry this practice can substantially increase the number of qualified prospects you receive from your referral sources. The amount does not have to be great, but it must be paid on time should the lead turn into a customer (client). Often a hand-written note or letter of thanks is just as meaningful and should be sent whether or not the referred prospect becomes a customer (client). A small token of appreciation (a potted plant or tickets to a ball game or concert) for those who consistently produce referrals can stimulate a steady stream of potential customers (clients).

Write down exactly what you will say when asking for a referral—be specific.

_____

_____

_____

_____

_____

GETTING REFERRALS (continued)

Track Your Referral Efforts

It is vital that you personally track the total number of referrals you produce and the success rates you achieve with each lead you receive even if your manager doesn't require you to. Tracking helps you to assess the worth of every referral source and the overall quality of the leads that they give you. It also keeps this vital source of business foremost in your mind so that asking for referrals becomes an unconscious habit.

Because only a small percentage of those you ask will be able to give you leads, there is a tendency for many sales representatives and service professionals to stop asking for referrals. However, by monitoring your progress you will begin to see how valuable this activity is to your sales success. Then you will want to improve your action plans and expand the process even further.

Lead Source Tracking

To help you keep track of your referral sources, you should set up a system similar to the following. Use 3" × 5" index cards if you want.

LEAD SOURCE:

Referral Name #1: _____

Contact: Yes: _____   No: _____

Outcome: _____

_____

Referral Name #2: _____

Contact: Yes: _____   No: _____

Outcome: _____

_____

JOIN INDUSTRY TRADE ASSOCIATIONS

If your customers (clients) are industry specific, become involved in their trade groups and associations. Many industry trade groups have associate memberships for suppliers to attract vendors to their annual convention as exhibitors. Sales and service professionals often become too involved with their own industry trade group or local sales association, at the expense of working with their customers' (clients') trade organizations. Since time is money, focus on working with your customers' (clients') trade associations before becoming heavily involved in your own.

What are the trade organizations that serve your customers (clients)?

_____

_____

_____

_____

Which ones are you currently involved in?

_____

_____

_____

_____

ACTIVELY PARTICIPATE IN THE GROUPS YOU JOIN

JOIN INDUSTRY TRADE ASSOCIATIONS (continued)

Joining Isn't Enough!

It takes more than joining a trade group to be successful. Become active enough to be selected to its committees and to work with its leadership. This means meeting with the decision makers of the various companies that belong to the group.

CASE STUDY: THE AWARD-WINNING WAY

Several years ago while working with a state innkeeper's association member this author received a special award for his efforts to promote this trade group and tourism throughout the state. The recognition produced a string of new clients not only from the association's membership, but from outside the industry as a result of the publicity created by the award. The innkeeper's association sent out a news release to many local, state and regional publications. They also wrote about his award and activity in their own monthly newsletter, distributed to all the hotels and motels in the state. From this publicity, the author was asked by the State Travel Council to design a statewide travel promotion. This work received so much national attention that the Virgin Islands territory government retained him to develop a promotion for their tourist attractions. He visited the islands, experienced all of the amenities they had to offer, and wrote a report. (He also received a handsome retainer for his work.)

Be Assertive

Trade groups often have difficulty obtaining help from their own members, a great opportunity for an enterprising professional to become actively involved in the organization. There is no guarantee that you will receive the recognition you deserve for your efforts, but do bring your work to the attention of key decision makers. Be assertive as you ask the association's leadership to assist you in meeting your sales objectives once you have gone the extra mile to help them.

Joining Other Organizations

Joining the organizations listed below might be as helpful in producing leads as joining your customers' (clients') trade associations.

▶ **The Chamber of Commerce**
In some industries, it is wise to join your local chamber of commerce small business association. Since your time is a valuable resource, when working with an industry association, chamber of commerce, small business group, service club or charity, make certain that the time spent in these organizations will generate prospects that can produce business. Usually there is a wide variety of firms represented, many of which could become customers (clients) once they learn about you and your products (services).

▶ **Service Clubs**
A service club is another place you can meet prospective customers or clients. Become actively involved to meet as many people as possible. If after a few months you find that the work you are doing does not justify the return, look for another club. Serving others is an important ideal, but remember, you can always serve others in a club that also provides you with prospects and referrals.

▶ **Charitable Organizations**
Charities that use "loaned executives" are often good sources for potential clients or referrals to potential clients. When you volunteer for a charity, assess the types of people who have also volunteered and determine how much time you will have to spend to cultivate leads from your service.

▶ **Political Party**
Becoming involved in a local political party can often produce sales in certain products (services). An insurance agent or attorney in a small town can get some great mileage out of being the mayor for a few terms. Getting involved in political campaigns can also help you meet many people. Getting elected to a school board or town council could help you gain a great reputation very quickly. Keep in mind that political activity is time consuming, often taking many months or even years to build up a reputation so that business begins to flow to you from your activity. But for certain professions (attorneys, insurance agents, bankers) and businesses (retail stores and shops, pharmacies,etc.), political activity could be an ideal way to generate leads.

JOIN INDUSTRY TRADE ASSOCIATIONS (continued)

► **Country Club or Sports Group**
Use your imagination. For every industry or trade group you can join, there is an equal number of social clubs that could assist you in developing prospects. Some professionals have learned they can produce leads even while enjoying their favorite recreational activity or hobby.

One financial service sales representative built his home adjacent to a country club that gave him reciprocal golfing privileges at similar clubs across the United States. He would invite top stockbrokers in a distant city to a golf outing at a prestigious golf club in their local community. After spending a day on the links, this professional had built enough rapport that the stockbrokers would enthusiastically sell his financial products to their clients.

What other organizations do you belong to that produce (or could produce) leads?

_____

_____

_____

_____

_____

Exercise: Become a Joiner

		YES	NO
1.	Do you know the trade organizations that serve your customers (clients)?	☐	☐
2.	Are you currently involved in any one of these organizations?	☐	☐
3.	If you are not involved, do you plan to join?	☐	☐
4.	Do you participate in the leadership of any of these trade organizations?	☐	☐
5.	If you haven't already, are you willing to join a committee?	☐	☐
6.	Do you feel you are as assertive as you can be in promoting your prospects to members of a trade group?	☐	☐

TRADE SHOWS CAN PAY BIG RETURNS

In many industries, trade shows are a cost-effective source of leads because potential customers (clients) come to you, rather than you having to find them. A valid criticism by some people is that working a trade show doesn't produce enough leads for the amount of time spent. To get the best results, take time to evaluate a show before you attend. If you exhibit primarily because a competitor has a display, you may be making a costly mistake. To be a valid promotional tool, a trade show must produce leads and, ultimately, sales.

Many able people fail to work a trade show properly. Top sales producers know that just passing out literature and answering questions will rarely develop qualified leads from even the best trade shows. Even though some trade organizations do not allow you to consummate a sale at the show, or the nature of your products or services may not make closing at the show feasible, your goal should be to produce qualified leads.

Trade Show Techniques

1. **Never make your primary activity at a trade show the distribution of sales literature.**
Research shows that most literature (85% to 95%) distributed at trade shows ends up in a waste can.

2. **Talk with and qualify as many attendees as possible** *as prospects, or obtain referrals from them.*

3. **Always arrange your booth so that you can sit down with prospects.**
Your goal is to bring people into your booth to discuss their needs, problems and the opportunities to work with them.

4. **Always place your literature at the back or side of your booth to draw prospects in so you can speak with them.**
Never set up your literature table in front of your booth for passersby to pick it up and walk away. A table in the front of an exhibit is a barrier to obtaining leads and making sales.

5. **Talk to everyone you meet at every function when you are away from the exhibit area.**

Just as many leads can be found around a snack bar or rest area as are generated by your booth.

6. **Qualify people at the show rather than just collecting calling cards from those you meet.**

Spend the time necessary to do screening or closing at the show.

7. **Ask everyone for referrals.**

Make certain you *ask specifically for the type of person you are seeking,* and whenever possible, *get permission to use the person's name* who gives you a referral.

CASE STUDY: TRADE SHOW SUCCESS STORY

When you work a trade show properly, the potential is staggering for writing orders and producing qualified leads. While working the National Superintendents of Schools Association convention in Atlantic City, New Jersey, one summer study abroad firm made the single largest sale it had ever recorded. The lead was cultivated at the snack bar with the superintendent of a large metropolitan school district. This educator would never have come to the foreign study exhibitor's booth because he was busy with association meetings and workshops. He had stopped to grab a snack, when a representative of the foreign study firm introduced himself. After the convention, the school district filled two (250-seat) jet airplanes with students who paid $1,250 each to learn French in France and Switzerland.

3

Find Prospects by Speaking and Writing

PREVIEW CHECKLIST

Before proceeding with this next section, check your prospecting knowledge.

	True	False
1. There are few topics proven suitable for seminar prospecting.	☐	☐
2. Tom Sawyer was a great salesperson.	☐	☐
3. Seminars are a very expensive way to prospect.	☐	☐
4. Teaching at a local college is an effective prospecting method because it gives you credibility.	☐	☐
5. Conducting joint seminars with attorneys or CPAs dilutes your credibility.	☐	☐
6. Writing a controversial letter to the editor is an effective prospecting method.	☐	☐
7. Research shows that sending clients regular newsletters is a waste of time and money.	☐	☐
8. To get an article published, you must refrain from referring to your product or service.	☐	☐
9. The biggest problem associated with prospecting seminars is that they often become social get-togethers.	☐	☐
10. A seminar can net at least thirty new clients.	☐	☐

Answers: 1. F 2. T 3. F 4. T 5. F 6. T 7. F 8. T 9. T 10. F

SPEAK OUT FOR LEADS

As you join trade groups to generate additional business, there often will be an opportunity to speak at their functions. Public speaking is not easy for people. Eighty-five percent of the executives surveyed in a recent study rated public speaking as their number-one fear. However, professionals who can speak well and entertain an audience are able to maximize their membership in trade groups and also generate leads by giving talks to other local groups and service clubs. Most program directors at service and social clubs have a difficult time finding entertaining speakers. They welcome the chance to work with a professional who has a topic that will appeal to and entertain their membership.

Creative Topics Generate Prospects

Not all products (services) have the fundamental elements that can provide a basis for an entertaining or educational address. However, for service professionals (attorneys, engineers, accountants, etc.), often a specialty area of your practice can develop into a talk that will attract attention, giving prospective clients a reason to seek out your services. Remember, before you reject the idea of public speaking based on the type of product (service) that you sell, you need to think creatively about this technique. Public speaking has many advantages in helping a professional search out qualified prospects. For example, a manufacturing process that reduces pollution can provide an interesting subject for discussion. A well-constructed talk on the environmental impact of your process could generate business from the right people and organizations. Here are a few ways you might generate prospects by speaking out:

► **Teach at a local college or university.**

   For certain professions this gives you exposure and credibility that you cannot obtain in any other way.

► **Radio and television talk shows.**

   Through persistence, one color consultant for the fashion industry secured a guest speaking engagement on a local women's TV program. From there she became a fashion consultant for the station and appeared regularly on programs that dealt with fashion trends. As a result of this exposure, she became the number-one color consultant in the world for the cosmetic and training organization that she represented.

► **Join a speakers' bureau.**

Work up several speeches and obtain regular bookings. Not only will you be paid for your efforts but this approach can, for the right industry and professions, produce a steady flow of business.

Exercise: Speaking Out for Leads

Brainstorm and list any other ways you can think of to generate prospects by speaking out.

_____

_____

_____

_____

_____

_____

_____

SPEAK OUT! PUBLIC SPEAKING CAN GENERATE QUALIFIED LEADS.

THE SECOND MOST POWERFUL PROSPECTING TOOL

Developing a seminar or workshop is the second most powerful prospecting tool available to a professional today. When you combine it with asking for referrals (to your seminar), it becomes *the most powerful prospecting* tool available because it multiplies your promotional capabilities by a factor of twenty or more. When you design an effective seminar, there is a mathematical certainty that you will end up with more customers (clients) than in a one-on-one selling approach. If your seminar or workshop has appeal, for every set of one thousand invitations you send, you should be able to generate a 1.5–3% response rate. Each mailing will thus recruit fifteen to thirty prospects.

Conducting Seminars:

- Puts you in the limelight as an expert.

- Enhances your image

- Jointly with other professionals (attorneys, financial planners, bankers) puts you in good company

- Helps to enhance your credibility

Seminars are also one of the most cost-effective promotions, due to the calculated approach used to produce qualified prospects. Workshops or seminars do not have to be an expensive proposition. Low-cost in-office presentations are all you need to be successful. Seminars and workshops can be a way of getting paid for prospecting.

Become an "Instant Expert"

Because most people are frightened to speak in front of a group, those who can speak often gain instant respect. Your audience immediately views you as an *expert* in your field and you gain credibility that you might not otherwise achieve as just a salesperson or service professional. And public speaking frequently produces an implied endorsement from the organization that engages you to speak. This too breaks down the barriers in the sales process and establishes additional credibility with those prospective customers (clients) that listen to your talk.

At a meeting of sixty-five bank marketing executives, representing approximately forty-five banking institutions, eleven of the participants sought out the keynote speaker to learn more about the services he provided for banking organizations. Six of the organizations became training or advisory service clients. His talk was not a pitch in any sense of the word. It simply gave attendees an overview of how a banking employee must cultivate specific selling skills to render high-quality customer service. Since the audience viewed the speaker as an expert, it was easy for him to close agreements with many of the bankers who inquired about his consulting services. Another favorable aspect of this speaking engagement was a handsome fee for his twenty-minute talk.

Prospecting Through Seminars

Prospecting through seminars is a successful promotional method for the following reasons:

► Your contacts may find it easier to give you referrals for a seminar than for a sales presentation because you are offering to give their leads some training, rather than just a sales pitch. Also, asking for a referral to a seminar is a *no pressure* request on your part.

► There are as many topics for seminars as there are types of prospects you seek for customers (clients).

► By structuring your seminar as a group learning experience, you lower a prospect's resistance to your sales presentation. People view your training as a nonthreatening social get-together. This helps open a prospect's mind to what you have to say and what you have to sell.

► As you develop effective training sessions, referrals from participants will expand your business geometrically.

Seminars are a professional way to build credibility. You can attract people who may never give you an appointment for a sales presentation. Make certain that your participants leave your workshop with solid information and good feelings.

THE SECOND MOST POWERFUL PROSPECTING TOOL (continued)

> ### *The Mark Twain Method of Marketing*
>
> The seminar approach is one of the best ways to apply the Mark Twain method of marketing. Some of the best sales training I ever received came at a very early age by a master salesman named Mark Twain (Samuel Clemens). The story he tells of Tom Sawyer whitewashing his aunt's fence illustrates Twain's insight into the sales process.
>
> Unaccustomed to working, Tom disliked the job immensely and realized that if his friends saw him working, he would lose his status as their leader. As his friends came closer, Tom began working extremely hard acting as if he enjoyed the job. Knowing Tom's attitude toward work, he astonished his friends by seeming to have a good time. After watching Tom work for a while, his friends asked if they might try to whitewash the fence. Tom made it seem as if he was the only one his aunt would allow to complete the work. Tom was having so much fun his friends begged him to whitewash the fence. Tom sat back, let them complete his work, and maintained his position as their leader. This is a great lesson for someone trying to learn how to sell, but there is one more element to the story that sets it apart as an exceptional sales analogy. Tom also made them pay him for the privilege of doing it.

Exercise: Seminar Prospecting

True False

1. ☐ ☐ Contacts are often more willing to give referrals to seminar leaders.

2. ☐ ☐ Seminar topics are limited, so only a select few qualify to lead them.

3. ☐ ☐ A prospect may feel threatened by seminar training and prefer a sales pitch.

4. ☐ ☐ Prospecting through seminars can help expand your business.

5. ☐ ☐ Seminars are a solid way to build respect and credibility in your field.

WRITE YOUR WAY TO PROSPECTING SUCCESS

Top professionals learn early in their careers the value of writing in producing qualified leads. In a busy sales schedule, a professional will often postpone writing projects for more pressing activities. Having developed a new sales reinforcement training program for the banking industry, this author sent the American Banker's Association a news release for the New Products column of their monthly magazine. Then the *ABA Journal* published a small article which netted me three or four inquiries about the training programs. However, almost a year later, an inquiry came in from a banking executive who had seen the article while going through back issues of the *ABA Journal*. My training firm established an ongoing instructional program with the bank that paid many times over the small amount of time spent writing the initial news release.

Put It on Paper

The following list of writing activities can produce a steady flow of business for your organization if you will only take the time to put some ideas down on paper:

1. **Write News Releases**—When something new happens in your organization, let the media know with a short news release. By using your imagination and creativity, you can find dozens of reasons to let newspapers, magazines, trade journals and other publications know about some aspect of your business. List some recent events in your company that could have been put into news releases.

_____

_____

_____

_____

WRITE YOUR WAY TO PROSPECTING SUCCESS (continued)

2. **Write a Newspaper or Magazine Article**—This takes more work than a news release, but it could pay off if the article is published with your byline and gives recognition to your company. As in public speaking, when you write a column, you are viewed as an expert, and this perceived expertise gives your readers the trust to seek you out and take advantage of what it is that you sell. List some potential article topics.

_____

_____

_____

_____

3. **Write Letters to the Editor**—If you stay close to your clients (customers), you will probably subscribe to their industry magazines or trade journals and, when possible, join their trade associations. As subjects come up in these industry publications that are appropriate for comment, you should take a stand and let your views be known about a topic, especially those that are controversial. Not everyone will agree with what you write, but at least half of the audience will find your arguments appealing, and some may even seek you out to transact some business. Like the other writing suggestions, this is an inexpensive way to put your name in front of many people. Some businesses or service organizations lend themselves well to editorializing, and some local papers will appreciate your comments. You have to be careful you don't overuse this source of free publicity, but an occasional letter to the editor could net you exposure you could not obtain in any other way. List any current or past issues about which you could have written to the editor.

_____

_____

_____

_____

4. **Write Trade Publication Articles**—Depending on your product (service) and your creativity, there could be an opportunity to write an article about a topic of interest to prospective customers (clients). To get your article published, you will have to refrain from promoting your products and services. But if the topic you chose to write about is timely, often people will call you because they see you as an expert. You are a published author, aren't you? Then their questions and interest can be turned into long-term business relationships. Reprints can then be made of the article, depending on the nature of the piece, and used as softeners to help prospective customers (clients) become more comfortable with you. What topics of interest could you develop into trade publication articles?

_____

_____

_____

_____

5. **Write a Book**—Royalty checks are nice, but I can honestly tell you that you will never get rich writing a book, unless you publish the next _One Minute Manager_ or _Gone with the Wind_. However, all the benefits suggested for writing news releases, articles and editorials accrue when you are a published author. Publishing not only helps to build your credibility with prospects and customers (clients), but it can give you exposure you might not attain any other way. List some possible book titles that describe the book your expertise would allow you to write.

_____

_____

_____

_____

WRITE YOUR WAY TO PROSPECTING SUCCESS (continued)

6. **Write Notes and Cards**—Whenever possible, write a personal note or get someone to help you write personal notes to make them special. This generates loyal customers (clients) and a steady stream of referrals. The reason it is so effective is that few professionals take the time to put something in writing. Joe Girard is considered by some as one of the greatest salespeople that ever lived. He was a car salesman in a Detroit dealership (some people refer to him as the dealer within the dealership). Joe Girard would consistently sell at least $2 million more than his nearest rival. No one was able to achieve his consistency. Joe Girard put out 18,000 pieces of mail a month. Constantly keep yourself in the minds of your customers and prospects by sending:

   - Thank you notes

   - Letters of congratulations or recognition

   - Birthday cards

   - Holiday cards

   - Anniversary cards

7. **Write Newsletters**—Some professionals regularly send out a newsletter to prospects and clients, but recent research shows that writing a newsletter is *not* an effective way to spend your time or money to attract new business. Most professionals, business leaders and consumers are inundated today with dozens of newsletters—from the local hospital trying to promote a wide variety of new services to the electric company teaching you how to save money on your electric bill. Most newsletters are never read because people feel they don't have the time. A more effective approach is to write a one-page broadcast letter with a headline that really grabs a prospect's attention. Sticking to one important topic, rather than putting out a four-page spread that no one takes the time to read, is a good way to attract interest and produce leads. List some possible one-page letter topics.

_____

_____

_____

_____

P A R T

4

Getting to
Decision Makers

PREVIEW CHECKLIST

Check how well you know how to get to decision makers.

	True	False
1. You should try to make a connection with a decision maker's boss.	☐	☐
2. The administrative assistant of the president of the company is a valuable business contact.	☐	☐
3. It is important to bring up your product or service as early as possible in your phone conversation with the decision maker.	☐	☐
4. Sometimes receptionists are trained to screen their boss' calls.	☐	☐
5. If your decision maker wants more information about your product or service, carefully explain over the phone what you can do to help him or her decide whether or not to meet with you.	☐	☐
6. Always follow up a phone conversation with a hand-written note of thanks.	☐	☐
7. It can take as many as five contacts to get an appointment with a decision maker.	☐	☐
8. An introductory letter to soften your contact is a good strategy.	☐	☐
9. A nice, professionally pre-printed label for envelopes makes a good first impression.	☐	☐
10. Don't take "no" responses from decision makers personally.	☐	☐

Answers: 1. T 2. T 3. F 4. T 5. F 6. T 7. F (5) 8. F 9. F 10. T

MAKING APPOINTMENTS WITH DECISION MAKERS

Whether you sell to consumers in their home or to executives at the highest corporate levels, you must make certain that you give your presentations to those prospects who *can* and *will* make a buying decision. Ineffective producers consistently fail to make contact with decision makers. In corporate prospecting, one of the best methods for finding the decision maker is to ask the receptionist to give you the name of the administrative assistant (write it down phonetically if it is difficult to pronounce) to the president of the company. Next, ask the president's or managing partner's administrative assistant to help you zero in on the person you need to meet in order to sell your product or service. Here is a formula that can help you get to the right person almost every time. To be most effective, put these ideas into your own words:

► Ask the receptionist for the name of the president's (or managing partner's) administrative assistant.

► When you speak to the administrative assistant, compliment him or her by suggesting that he or she probably has extensive knowledge of the organization and its personnel. Then, ask for the name of the decision maker. For example:

> *Terry? Jordan Jones calling from the Widget Corporation of America. So that I don't disrupt your company trying to find just the right person, I thought I'd speak with you first. I've found that the president's administrative assistant usually knows just about everything that is going on in a company. I'm trying to locate the person who makes the final decision on widgets to send some promotional materials and also see if I can schedule an appointment. Could you please tell me who in your company makes these decisions?*

► After you are given the name of the person, ask for the name of the decision maker's boss. You won't always get cooperation, but most times you will receive the name of the person who can tell you what you need to know.

> *Who does Dana Lin (the decision maker) report to, Terry?* (Use the assistant's name as often as you can without sounding stilted or condescending.)

► Next, send a softening letter to the decision maker's boss (see the section below about softening) with a note that you will be calling soon for an appointment. (From this point forward, you can use the scenario outlined below for either contacting the decision maker or the boss. Many times the boss will pass you off by suggesting that you speak directly with the decision maker and will even make an introduction for you. If this happens, you are most likely contacting the right person.)

► The day that your softening letter arrives, or no later than the day after, call the decision maker's boss for an appointment. Use the following appointment script to set up a meeting (this script will work for making an appointment with the decision maker as well):

- Start by using the supervisor's or decision maker's first name as a question.

  Pat?

- Next introduce yourself using your full name.

  This is Avery Doran calling.

- If this is a referral, state who suggested that you call. If you received the name from someone other than the president's administrative assistant, use that name. If not, use the assistant's name.

  Terry Larsen suggested that I call you.

- Tell the boss or the decision maker the reason for your call. Give a good reason for spending time with you. (Appealing to cost-effectiveness usually is the best approach.)

  Pat, I'm calling to tell you how your firm can save thousands of dollars on your next purchase of widgets.

- Next, use a provocative question to gain attention. This hypothetical question sets the stage for asking for an appointment. (Memorize these three power words.)

  *Pat, **if you felt** . . .*

- To complete the provocative question, use two, or no more than three customer (client) benefits to round out the question.

  . . . You could (1) save thousands of dollars off the base price of our new widgets, (2) reduce your delivery times and (3) save money on all widget delivery charges . . .

MAKING APPOINTMENTS WITH DECISION MAKERS (continued)

- Then tell your prospect that you will take only a few minutes to demonstrate how to obtain the benefits.

  . . . would you spend fifteen or twenty minutes to learn how you can obtain these lower prices?

- If there is interest, use an "either-or close."

  Pat, would Monday at 2:00 PM or Wednesday at 9:00 AM be best for you?

- If the response is "Tell me more about it," you need to side-step this stall. Just say:

  It's difficult on the phone . . . I really need to demonstrate our widgets and the savings we can offer from information you give to me . . . I promise not to take more than twenty minutes.

- What do you say if the decision maker says, "No!" (Eighty to ninety percent of your calls will be answered "no" the first time you ask.) Just say:

  No problem!

- No matter what is said, just say:

  No problem!

- Then give your prospect another reason for spending time with you. Promise a second time that you will take no more than 20 minutes.

  Pat, I promise I'll take no more than twenty minutes to demonstrate how your firm can achieve great cost savings on your next order of widgets.

> **Note:** Statistics show that if you only ask for an appointment once, you will average a 10% to 15% closing rate. If you consistently ask for an appointment at least twice, your closing rate will improve 30% to 40%. Ask three times and you can consistently achieve a 60% or higher appointment-closing ratio.

► A decision maker's boss will usually suggest that you speak with the decision maker directly. When this happens, ask him or her to connect you with the person you need to see. This procedure will often give the decision maker the impression that the boss wants him or her to see you. This perception helps make your initial call much easier than the normal cold call.

► If it is inconvenient for the decision maker to speak with you, or if the decision maker is out of the office when the boss makes the referral call, thank the boss and state that you will get in touch with the decision maker later.

► Because you may end up meeting with the boss at a later date, send a handwritten note of thanks to make a positive impression.

► When you finally make your appointment call to the decision maker, use the boss's name as the person who suggested that you call. This is one of the best referral sources a salesperson can cultivate.

► In some companies you can go two levels above the decision maker to generate an appointment. If the president's administrative assistant is wrong about who makes the decision, by speaking with a decision maker's boss you will rarely call on someone that is not in a position to purchase your products or services.

Soften Often

Since it takes an *average* of nine contacts or impressions before you can effectively close a sale, follow this strategy:

> Before calling the decision maker or the boss, first send a softening letter to set the stage for your appointment call. Remember that the sale you are trying to make is for an appointment. *Never try to sell your products or services in your softening letter or on the phone.*

> Whenever you obtain a referral, make certain that your prospect knows that this person told you to make contact.

> No matter what type of communication you make with a prospect, always give the person a reason for spending time with you.

The following will give you an idea of how you might set the stage for obtaining an appointment with a softening letter.

MAKING APPOINTMENTS WITH DECISION MAKERS (continued)

The Selling Edge® Approach

Be creative in finding ways to make an impression on your prospective customer (client). Sales representatives at The $elling Edge® use a puzzle either before appointment calls (this usually goes before the softening letter) or just after appointment calls to give a second impression. They often turn the puzzle over and write a short note on the back. If the decision maker came as a referral, the note might say something like: "Dana Lin suggested that I contact you. I'll be in touch in a day or two," and then sign it.

To make certain this softener gets to the decision maker:

- break the puzzle up

- put it into a small, odd-sized envelope

- hand address the envelope

- use a commemorative stamp

When feeling and seeing the envelope, it will be viewed as personal correspondence and not screened out. Rarely in the beginning stages of developing a relationship should you use labels or typewritten addresses. Hand-addressed plain envelopes seem to get more attention and will help you to make more appointments.

After the puzzle and softening letter is the telephone call to make the appointment. Sometimes, however, it is difficult to make an appointment because office personnel have been told to screen out certain types of calls. It is important to remember to treat these people with courtesy and *never try to get around the decision maker's administrative assistant*. If your technique works and is found out, you will never make a sale at that organization as long as that person is there to block your approach.

Working with "Screeners"

The best approach to getting around administrative assistants or anyone required to screen phone calls is to never try. Instead, work with them and "sell" them on helping you to get through to the boss. You can use a variation of the technique outlined above. Keep in mind that these people want to do the best job they can for their boss and their company. You merely need to build on this desire—give them some personal benefits for helping you achieve your objective.

For situations where the assistant does not respond positively, try calling your decision maker before normal work hours or during lunch on the chance that the boss will pick up the phone.

Exercise: Get Creative

Think of some creative ways to approach the first prospecting contacts (i.e., a puzzle or softening letter)

_____

_____

_____

✓ Ask a friend or family member to role-play phone conversations with you.

✓ Alternate roles. By playing the alternate role you may learn a new approach.

CALL OFTEN

When you make a prospecting call you are intruding into the daily activities of the person you are trying to contact. If they are having a good day there is a chance your message will be heard. You might call at a bad time when the person is disagreeable because of other circumstances beyond your control.

Remember:

- Don't take a negative response personally.

- Put the prospect's name back into your list of prospects to contact again in two or three months.

- Try a different approach to obtaining an appointment on your next contact.

- Persistence pays big dividends. Usually it takes three or four telephone calls before you can determine the true feelings of a suspect. In some cases, you might make twenty calls before you are able to obtain an appointment, based on the conversation that transpires on each call. Do not waste time with people who have no interest, but don't set an arbitrary cutoff either.

Use the Right-Ear Technique

A proven technique to avoid call reluctance when making appointments is based on brain dominance. The left side of the brain is analytical while the right side is more emotional and creative. Most right-handed people hold the telephone to their left ear so their right hand is free to take notes and perform computer functions. However, by holding the telephone to the left ear, all the negative responses are absorbed in the emotional side of your brain. This in turn, produces negative feelings about prospecting calls and makes it more difficult to make those calls that are necessary to succeed at the numbers game.

Research in telemarketing organizations has found that the right-ear technique improved their sales and appointment success ratios significantly. If you use a headset, make certain that the sound comes in only on the right side.

Exercise: Phone Log Record

Try keeping a log of attempted phone calls. Record the time and day of each call and the response, positive or negative, each time you called. Try calling the same place on different days and times. Record any changes in response.

P A R T

5

Time and Contact Management

PREVIEW CHECKLIST

How are your time-management skills?

	True	False
1. Friday is often a good day to get appointments with decision makers.	☐	☐
2. One hour is the most effective length for your presentation.	☐	☐
3. Monday is a very productive day to hold appointments.	☐	☐
4. If you spend a lot of time on the phone, take a break every four hours.	☐	☐
5. Don't discount the possibility of prospecting before or after typical business hours.	☐	☐
6. Use a map to plan the most efficient route for your appointments to avoid dead time.	☐	☐
7. Investing in a software prospect-tracking program is a good decision.	☐	☐
8. The biggest drawback to software tracking programs is that they are too generic.	☐	☐
9. Make notes while speaking to prospects to ensure complete and accurate information.	☐	☐
10. You should try to get at least 20 appointments per week.	☐	☐

Answers: 1. F 2. F (20 min.) 3. T 4. F (2 hours) 5. T 6. T 7. T 8. F 9. T 10. F (40 appointments)

HOW TO WIN AT THE NUMBERS GAME

To win at the numbers game, top professionals learn to make presentations (at least on their initial call) in twenty to forty minutes flat. Then they find the location of their next appointment or make several prospecting telephone calls before their next meeting. Many sales people fail at the numbers game because they think that in an effective sale, they must tell their prospect everything they know about their product (service). A typical sales call usually runs well over an hour and a half, cutting down on the total number of calls that can be made on a given day.

Top professionals know that most people have an attention span of about fifteen or twenty minutes. They develop a consultative presentation based on a contact's needs and attention span. This sales approach allows them to meet with more potential customers (clients) than the average sales person. It also gives them an edge in the selling game that is hard for nonproducers to understand or execute.

Make appointments at least one week in advance.

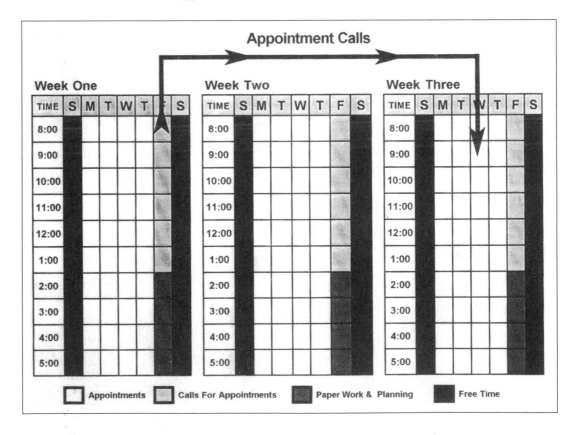

Once you learn how to make a sales presentation in twenty to forty minutes, it is easy to schedule ten or more sales calls per day. Begin making calls at 8:00 A.M. (or even earlier, for breakfast, in some industries) and keep seeing prospects into the early evening hours. Even if you are not a "morning person," there are people who like to start their day before many of us are even awake. Also remember, there are decision makers who are workaholics who never seem to leave the job. You can contact these people in the early evening long after other workers have gone home for the night.

Monday is the best day to both make and hold appointments. Friday is the least productive day for both, because decision makers tend to start their weekend earlier than other employees. Since it is more important for you to use the good days for in-person appointments, schedule Friday morning for appointment calls, even though it won't be the most productive calling session, rather than a day when you should be seeing decision makers.

Try to make appointments at least a week in advance, so you can take advantage of a more open schedule with prospects than if you try to call on a Friday for appointments during the following week.

Telemarketing research shows that after two hours on the phone, productivity dramatically declines.

- Take a good break after your first two hours.

- Do some paperwork or map planning for future appointment calls before your second session.

- Never try to call for more than four hours in a single day.

Call from 8:30 to 10:30 A.M., just before lunch, or at 4:30 P.M. Schedule the rest of your time for paperwork or additional map planning. Keep your weekends as free as possible from work activities. Sales is a highly stressful job, and you need the free time to rejuvenate. If you work according to the plan outlined in this manual, you'll rarely need to work weekends.

REDESIGN AND REDEFINE YOUR WEEK

THE EIGHT-"DAY," FORTY-APPOINTMENT WEEK

Psychologists tell us that breaking projects or processes down into small chunks helps to make big jobs easier and more palatable. The following ideas will help you prospect effectively and see dramatic sales success in the process.

The eight-"day," forty-appointment week can systematically put you in front of more decision makers than typical calling plans. Since the average sales representative or service professional will make only three to five appointment calls a day, top professionals double this number by chunking their day into two sessions of five one-hour slots, which they treat as a full "day." This gives them an eight-"day" sales week (Monday through Thursday) covering forty appointment slots.

The *goal* of the eight-"day," forty appointment week is to work each day to come as close as possible to 40 appointments, strive for at least 20 appointments—or more—each week and by keeping each appointment to no more than 20 minutes, the salesperson has time for pre- and post-appointment paperwork. Service professionals who have other jobs or work at sales part-time may need to alter these numbers to meet their needs and schedule.

Chunk to achieve success. Break days into two segments.

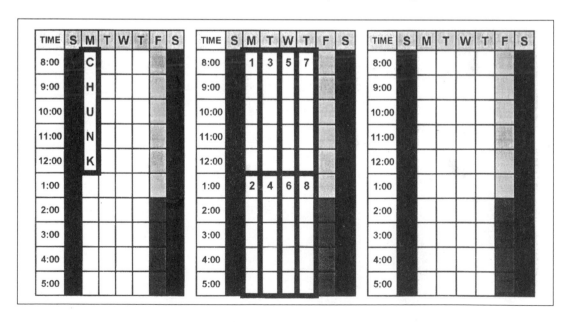

If decision makers are not available during the times you have openings, make appointments further in the future so that you maintain schedule efficiency and start to build up your appointment base in the numbers game. (Often professionals make the mistake of thanking their prospects then suggesting that they call back later, rather than setting a distant appointment at the first call.) Depending on your industry or profession, a four-hour Friday calling schedule should produce ten to fifteen appointments. Some days, however, it is easier to make appointments than others. There is really no explanation for this.

Friday prospecting calls can average ten to fifteen appointments.

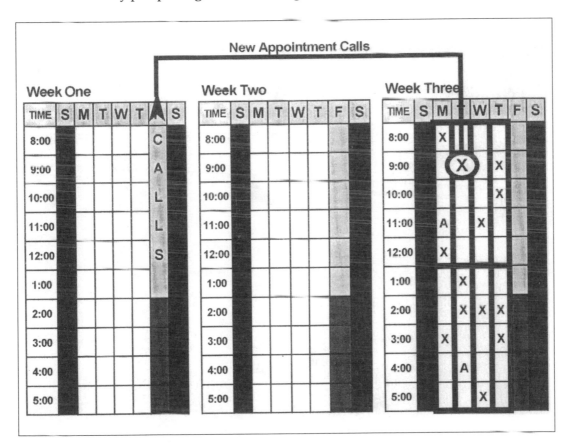

THE EIGHT-"DAY" FORTY-APPOINTMENT WEEK (continued)

Use That Pay Phone

There is an important prospecting technique to help you win the numbers game. To improve your track record, carry a pocket full of dimes and quarters to use in a pay phone for prospecting between field calls. This system is simple and effective. After completing a sales call and locating your next meeting, find a pay phone to fill in the blank spaces in your appointment schedule. It is even better if you have access to a cellular phone. The telephone can pay big dividends if you use it to its full advantage in the field.

Fill in appointment openings as you make your sales call.

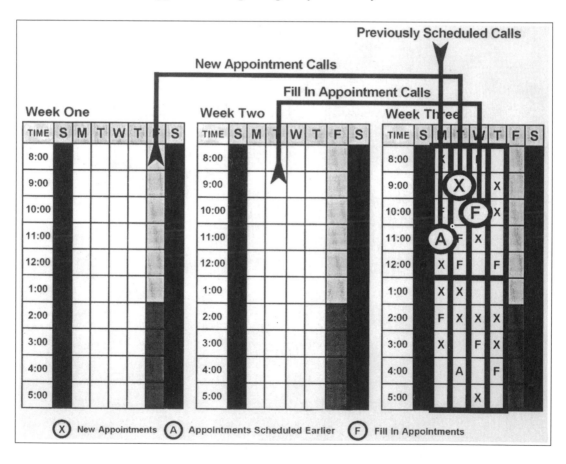

Map Planning

Top sales producers adhere to the adage *If you fail to plan, you plan to fail.* An important element in making solid prospecting calls is sound map planning combined with systematic appointment scheduling. Map planning is important in helping a sales or service professional make the one or two extra calls a day that mean a consistently higher sales rate. Map planning is a simple process of plotting the locations of your suspects, prospects and customers (clients) on a map so that, as you call for appointments, you keep your sales calls blocked in a specific section of the city and reduce travel time between appointments.

You first need to develop an efficient territory routing map on which you have marked the locations of your A, B and C prospects. Next, plot key points like your office, home, shipping points (if applicable), and some major customers (clients) from which you can start your sales day. Then take a good look at which routes are best for efficiently covering your territory.

How to Create and Improve Routing Plans

Here are some suggestions that will help improve your present route pattern or establish new ones.

1. Focus on territories where you have the best opportunities for increased business—where you have customers and A-rated prospects.

2. Divide your territory into sectors and reduce your driving time during *prime contact* hours. One thing to do during noncontact hours, of course, is to drive from home to the first appointment in the morning and home from the last one at night. Good routing will keep your dead time to a minimum.

3. Even within a sector, reduce your driving time and maximize the number of contacts each day by using looping driving patterns. Start out each day with contacts nearby. Then drive to ones progressively further away on a loop that brings you back to other contacts later in the day.

4. You might select a hotel or restaurant as a pit stop, as well as for telephoning and checking for messages as you work a given sector of your territory.

5. Keep your regular routing plans flexible so you can change course as new selling opportunities arise.

Exercise: Managing Your Time

Checklist

Place a check next to the items which are true for you on a regular basis.

_____ **1.** I strive to provide a concise 15- to 20-minute consultative presentation.

_____ **2.** I use the early morning hours to make the majority of my appointment calls.

_____ **3.** I try to follow the "eight-day," forty appointment week approach.

_____ **4.** I use pay phones or a cellular phone to make calls between appointments.

_____ **5.** I use map planning to cut down on travel time.

Re-evaluate those items you did not check and try to incorporate them into your day-to-day activities.

TRACKING YOUR EFFORTS

Once you sense how difficult it is to manage all the sales leads you can generate using the ideas outlined in this book, you will try to develop a systematic method for tracking each new prospect. The following form and the methods for using it make up the best manual system for tracking leads. Photocopy this form as it is, or copy it front and back and cut it in half to fit in most standard-sized day planners.

As you speak with a prospect (by phone or in person), use the form to make notes about your conversation. Fill out as much of the form as possible after the interview has ended, including:

- Your impressions

- The products you have discussed or sold

- A specific date for follow-through (critical to reaching out for more business)

Next, record the prospect's last name and first initial on your daily planner or calendar on the specific day you have planned for follow-through. Then write the letters "AF" in parentheses next to the prospect's last name to remind you that the information on this lead is located in your alphabetical file (a file folder, accordion file, or binder).

Once you have listed the prospect in your planner or on a calendar, save time by filing the Prospect Follow-Through Form in your alphabetical file under the first letter of the prospect's last name. Most people are able to locate files just as quickly when they are in the right alphabetical letter group, regardless of whether you alphabetize each form within the letter group. On the day the prospect's name shows up on your day planner or calendar, locate the client's Follow-Through Form in your alphabetical file and decide what action to take.

This system for tracking prospects is thorough and efficient. The key to its success, as with all the techniques you have learned thus far, is in the amount of effort you put forth to make this system a part of your daily work habits.

PROSPECT FOLLOWTHROUGH FORM

Rating
A B C

Individual Background

Name: _____

Company: _____

Address: _____

City: _____ State: _____ Zip: _____

Business Phone: _____ Home Phone: _____

Other Information: _____

Products/Services/Problems

Discussed: _____

Followthrough Action

DATE	ACTIVITY DESCRIPTION	COMPLETED (✔)

DATE	ACTIVITY DESCRIPTION	COMPLETED (✔)

Notes:

Use a Computer Tracking System

There are over 140 specialized database managers designed to assist professionals in tracking the promotional activities of their prospects and customers (clients). Many computer tracking programs are generic, while some are industry specific, such as those designed to help stockbrokers and insurance agents track their leads and clients.

Research by *Sales & Marketing Management* magazine suggests that when a company computerizes the sales-tracking process, there is an average sales productivity increase of over 43 percent. This productivity gain is no mystery when you understand how well computerized tracking systems work. Many of these programs have a one-button telephone dialing feature that takes the drudgery out of making call-backs. You are up and running in seconds and can use small blocks of time to expand the number of calls you make each day. Tracking software manages detailed information on each contact, making specific data available at the touch of a key. Most have tickler devices based on the next contact date that make it almost impossible for you to forget to get back to someone (unless you forget to turn on your computer). Some tracking software also includes a personal management system, with calendars, to-do lists and daily phone logs.

Often, tracking software has a text editor or word-processing capability that allows you to pull up a series of form letters at the end of a call. This feature helps you to soften your contacts or send written confirmations for appointments with little effort. The costs of computers are coming down to the point where most people can afford one, even if their firm will not fund the purchase. Along with the ability to track more efficiently and effectively, the word-processing capability can make the purchase of hardware and software a solid investment by efficiently producing the qualified leads needed for consistent sales success.

PROSPECTING REVIEW

Business and sales professionals can win in the numbers game by being successful in prospecting. Understanding the importance of prospecting, and making use of the available tools are essential. Below is a review checklist of the tools and techniques that help ensure success.

► **Make Use of Published Material**
- The Yellow Pages
- Business directories
- Trade publications
- Mailing lists

► **Explore Networking Possibilities**
- Become a member of the Chamber of Commerce
- Join social organizations
- Communicate with associates
- Participate in trade shows
- Conduct a seminar

► **Write and Publish**
- Cards, notes and letters
- Newsletters
- Magazine or newspaper articles
- Trade publications
- Books

► **Make Appointments**
- See professionals with decision-making and buying power

► **Manage Time Efficiently**
- Follow the eight-"day," forty appointment week plan
- Use map planning
- Track and record details of phone conversations and appointments
- Use new computer technology

PART

6

Appendix

REFERENCE MATERIAL

Here is a small sampling of a few good reference works that may be available in the business section of your local library. You can use these reference tools to locate decision makers that will have an interest in your products or services:

Published Materials

1. The *Cole Directory*, listing over 1,200 American cities, gives information about buying power in residential neighborhoods, street directories, an office building directory, a numerical telephone guide and a real estate section. It also has a prospecting system for business contacts.

2. The *Directory of Industrial Data Sources* is a detailed listing of information sources on many different industries.

3. The *Dun & Bradstreet Million Dollar Directory* lists companies that have a net worth of over $1 million and the names of the companies' top officers. Dun & Bradstreet has also published a second volume that lists companies with a net worth from $500,000 to $1 million.

4. The *Dun & Bradstreet's State Sales Guide* is a series listing businesses operating in each state. It also provides information including credit ratings, phone numbers and years in business.

   Dun & Bradstreet publishes directories on such topics as corporate management, business ranking guides, and Dun's market identifier, as well as many others.

5. *Moody's Investor Service* produces a variety of handbooks which you might find of value. Their investor fact sheet, for example, has a description of over 4,000 publicly held companies. It includes stock information, sales by line of business, financial information and a summary of current news about each listed company.

6. Crisscross directories, also called reverse directories, list telephone numbers by street and house number. They then provide a person's name or company name and phone number. This source for leads allows you to prospect in specific areas of a city where you think you might find the right type of person for your products or services. An obvious use for this directory is in locating just the right socioeconomic condition, interest group or age bracket since people tend to congregate based on these conditions.

7. The *Directory of Associations,* compiled by the Gale Research Company, is a directory of all major trade association meetings. It contains locations and dates so you can keep abreast of trade shows and conferences attended by your customers (clients).

8. The *Standard & Poor's Register of Corporations, Directors and Executives* gives names and personal information of over 100,000 key people in a variety of small, medium and large corporations. It lists corporate officers, directors, partners and principals, giving information on corporate position, college affiliations, residence data and more.

9. The *Thomas Register of American Manufacturers* is a massive work that lists large and small firms under an alphabetical product heading. A rating of a company's capital gives you some idea of the size of each of the firms. Volumes 1–12 of the *Register* list products and services. Volumes 13 and 14 contain company profiles including names, addresses, branch offices and officers. Volumes 15–21 are catalog files showing full-page advertisements of listed companies with detailed information.

10. *Who's Who* is a directory that gives a brief biography of thousands of important individuals from many walks of life, listing information about the honors and awards they have received, schools attended, positions held and more.

11. U. S. Government Printing Office
Washington, DC 20402
(202) 738-3238

Mailing List Brokers

The following are brokers who have a good reputation:

A-Caldwell & Company
4350 Georgetown Square
Atlanta, GA 30338
(800) 241-7425

Aldta
7000 151st Street
Apple Valley, MN 55124
(800) 331-7410

American Business Lists
5711 South 86th Circle
Omaha, NB 68127
(800) 336-8349

Brooks Mann
1360 West 9th Street, Suite 230
Cleveland, OH 44130
(216) 696-5588

Dun & Bradstreet
3 Sylvan Way
Parsipany, NJ 07054
(201) 605-6000

Eatna National List Company
579 First Bank Drive, Suite 230
Palatine, IL 60067
(800) 621-2392

Hugo Dunhill Mailing Lists
630 Third Avenue
New York, NY 10017
(800) 223-6454

BIBLIOGRAPHY

Covey, Steven R. *The Seven Habits of Highly Effective People*. New York: Simon & Schuster, 1989.

Edwards, Betty. *Drawing on the Right Side of the Brain*. New York: Tarcher Perigee/Putman, 1989.

Evered, James F. *The Disciplines of Selling: A Motivational Approach*. Denton, TX: Fefco Publishing, 1986.

Hanlorn, Al. *Creative Selling Through Trade Shows*. New York: Hawthorn Books, 1977.

Ley, D. Forbes. *The Best Seller*. New Port Beach, CA: Sales Success Press, 1984.

McCaffrey, Mike with Jerry Derloskon. *Personal Marketing Strategies: How to Sell Yourself, Your Idea, and Your Services*. Englewood Cliffs, NJ: Prentice-Hall, 1983.

Mitchel, Gary. *The Heart of the Sale*. New York: Amacom-American Management Association, 1991.

Nixon, H. K. *Principles of Selling*. New York: McGraw-Hill, 1931, 1942.

Pacetta, Frank with Roger Gittines. *Don't Fire Them, Fire Them Up—A Maverick's Guide to Motivating Yourself and Your Team*. New York: Simon & Schuster, 1994.

Shook, Robert L. *Ten Greatest Salespersons: What They Say About Selling*. New York: Harper & Row, 1978.

Shook, Robert L. *The Lacy Techniques of Salesmanship*. New York: Dow Jones-Irwin, 1971, 1982.

Taylor, Robert F. *Back to Basics Selling*. New York: Prentice-Hall, 1985.

Willingham, Ron. *The Best Seller: The New Psychology of Selling and Persuading People*. Englewood Cliffs, NJ: Prentice-Hall, 1984.

OVER 150 BOOKS AND 35 VIDEOS AVAILABLE IN THE 50-MINUTE SERIES

50-Minute Series Books and Videos Subject Areas . . .

Management
Training
Human Resources
Customer Service and Sales Training
Communications
Small Business and Financial Planning
Creativity
Personal Development
Wellness
Adult Literacy and Learning
Career, Retirement and Life Planning

Other titles available from Crisp Publications in these categories

Crisp Computer Series
The Crisp Small Business & Entrepreneurship Series
Quick Read Series
Management
Personal Development
Retirement Planning